Firmament

Poems by

Kathleen L. Housley

Higganum Hill Books : Higganum, Connecticut

First Edition
First Printing May 1, 2007

Higganum Hill Books
P.O. Box 666, Higganum, CT 06441
Phone (860) 345-4103
Email: rcdebold@mindspring.com

Library of Congress Control Number: 2006100911
ISBN10: 0-9776556-3-6
ISBN13: 978-0-9776556-3-2
Cover image: *Christ to heaven_april.* ©*2006* Francis Trottier All rights reserved.
Used by Permission
The fractal images ©2006 Paul Bourke and colleagues, cf. Acknowledgements.
All rights reserved. Used by permission.

Library of Congress Cataloging-in-Publication Data

Housley, Kathleen L.
  Firmament : poems / by Kathleen L. Housley. -- 1st ed.
     p. cm.
  ISBN 978-0-9776556-3-2 (alk. paper)
  I. Title.
  PS3608.O8644F57 2007
  811'.6--dc22
                          2006100911

Independent Publishers Group distributes Higganum Hill Books.
Phone: (800) 888-4741   www.ipgbook.com
Printed in the United States of America.

Dedication

To my husband Tim, a biologist who is both a skeptic and a true believer, for whom life at the cellular level is as beautiful as the stars in the heavens.

Acknowledgments

Grieving Knows No Dearth in its Verdant Season
The Fool Jots Down a Bedtime Prayer
Wrestling With an Angel
Apostate
The Magi
The Sistine (renamed Adam)
    The Christian Century
Adam Dreams of Darwin's Finch
Babel
Cartographer of Disaster
Lessons for a Young God
    Snakes
    Chimera
    Grasses
        Image
Black Tea
    Terra Nova, MIT Press
Riverbed,
    New Hope International: An Anthology of Little Press Poets
(England)
Coming to Terms
    The Climbing Art
Wind
Heavens
    Nimble Spirit Online (nimblespirit.com)

Grateful thanks to Paul Bourke, University of Western Australia, and his colleagues, Cliff Pickover, Andrew Wayne Graff, and Roger Bagula, for their kind permission to use the Fractal Graphics.

Contents

Lessons for a Young God

The Hidden

Parched Wilderness

Void and Vault

Consider Thy Heavens

"The heavens are telling the glory of God and the firmament proclaims his handiwork."

Psalm 19: 1

Lessons for a Young God

"Whom did the Lord consult to enlighten him,
and who taught him the right way?" Isaiah 40: 14

Clifford Attractor

Gauze-like in its delicacy, the fractal moves inward and outward.

THE MAGI

We kick our camels' sides and curse, but they refuse to rise,
as if this house were the only oasis in a trackless desert,
and this child, playing in the doorway, the owner of the well.
They swing their ponderous heads slowly from side to side.
Their silver harness bells tinkle, their vermillion tassels flap,
and the child laughs.

He cannot be the one foretold to lead us to the abode of light,
where wisdom glistens like dewdrops on which new worlds curve.
We must have misread the astrological signs or been dazzled
by a wind-driven spark. But how do we explain the strange behavior
of our beasts? They stretch out their necks on the sand and sigh.
It sounds like prayer.

There being none other, we may as well present our gifts to him,
although they feel all wrong, as if we had carried precious salt
across steep mountain passes to offer to a prince living by the sea.
Worthless to us, we will leave our frankincense to purchase bread,
and our gold to pay for lessons. Of what use is myrrh? Before we go,
let us buy him a ball.

Far away, we perceive our granddaughters twirling prayer wheels.
Through our minds' sanctum echoes the sound of ripe plums tumbling
into beggars' bowls. In the ravine of the roan horse, lightning blasts
a single tree. Like closed pine cones, our hearts burst open in the heat!
We would not be more astonished if a star slipped from the night
to hover here beyond the dawn.

Too stunned to dismount, we gaze and gaze. How extraordinary!
The ordinary child!

Lessons for a Young God

Snakes

*"The infant shall play over the hole of the cobra,
and the young child dance over the viper's nest."* Isaiah 11: 8

Death Adder
> Why does the child play above our dens,
> lifting our brood in his hands like toys?
> Have the ones who strike us with mattocks
> not warned him of our venom?

Sidewinder
> He gallops his carved animals
> to the edges of our nests,
> too little to know how simple
> it is for us to pierce his side.

Horned Viper
> Yet we sense in our cold skins
> the warmth of his hands against the Earth,
> flooding us with a strange compassion,
> as if all the seas have overflowed their beds.

Asp
> If he is to become shepherd of the frightened,
> he must himself feel time's fangs.
> Let the beginning of his wisdom
> be our reverent gift of fear.

Water Moccasin
> First we will teach him to watch
> from the periphery of his eyes
> for the slight ripple in the saw grass,
> the zigzag through the watercress,

Naja Naja
> the blink of pattern among green leaves,
> the mottled shade in a shale wall,
> the shadow sliding beneath
> closed doors at dusk.

Green Mamba
>Then we will train him to identify
>the upright ones who coil questions,
>injecting the slow poison of doubt
>for which there is no antidote.

Copperhead
>And when he learns all there is to know
>and leaves this holy mountain,
>we will wait for the day
>he returns,
>
>at last to twine peaceably around his arms:
>brothers to the mongoose, sisters to the eagle.

Lessons for a Young God

Chimera

"And you, son of man, hear what I say to you:
you shall not be a contradiction
as are the children of contradiction." Ezekiel 2: 8

We are Ezekiel's dream creature
reflected in the waters of exile:
human, lion, eagle, ox,
moving all directions
on wheels within wheels;
seeing all things
from rims encrusted with eyes;
holding aloft a sheet of ice
on which blazes sacred fire.

Seeking the One, we have traced
the leviathan's white wake
across storm-churned waters.
The nightjar threaded us a path
beyond snowy mountains.
Our shadow has glided
back and forth over the face
of the world for eons,
watching and listening.

But the child we have found,
at last, is like us: a chimera,
part fierce Lion of Israel,
part gentle Lamb of God.

Now we must help him
meld his warring parts,
for all things are possible
to him who is all things,
but not all things are good.

We will show him how to be
a farmer who can plow a cliff face
with a yoke of falcons, and a warrior
who can rock an infant to sleep.

Perhaps then, when he grows up,
he will possess the wisdom
to become a fisherman who trolls
for humans without hook or net,
or a king who washes feet.

Our pinions quiver with joy
as we lift him up.
How heavy he is!
How light!

Wolves

"The wolf shall live with the lamb."

Isaiah 11: 6a

The boy destined to shepherd wolves
shall lead us to green pastures
where sheep unsafely graze —
guide us by still waters in valleys
where we are the shadows of death —
prepare a table before us
on which he himself lies down.

Lessons for a Young God

Grass

*"He grew up before the Lord like a young plant
whose roots are in parched earth." Isaiah 53: 2*

What is it for which the child waits
at the fold of these dry hills, crouched
beside a river of sand that holds
the pattern of flowing water?
Nothing is alive here but our seeds
rattled from their cases by the wind,
thirsty for a second coming of the rain.

Perhaps the boy is like a small stone
tumbled downstream by a cloudburst,
never to return to the land of moist things.
Yet as we arch our brittle stalks overhead,
attempting to protect him from the sun,
we sense a subterranean reservoir,
pure and deep, toward which our roots bend.

All day we rustle into his listening heart
our knowledge of spate and drought,
of torrents that force a desert to bloom
only to vanish into the earth, leaving us
to wither and die. But we also whisper
of a spring hidden in the shade of a rock
where the wild goats come to drink.

At night he curls up like a seed sprout,
while around him we sing lullabies
of green hosannas in our hollow stems.

Lessons for a Young God

Wind

"And he shall be shelter from tempest.
refuge from storm,
an ever-flowing stream in dry ground,
a shadow of a great rock in a thirsty land."
Isaiah 32: 2

It is for me, essence of spirit and breath,
to help the child comprehend his names,
foretold in metaphor's multiple tongues,
with worlds within each unmarked vowel.

> Blown north, *Shelter from tempest* shall sail
> a small skin-boat through steep, cold seas.

> Twirled west, *Refuge from storm* shall trace
> the path of the moon in the dust of the kiva floor.

> Driven south, *Ever-flowing stream* shall carry water
> in an ostrich shell across the Kalahari Desert.

> Blasted east, *Shadow of a great rock in a thirsty land*
> shall learn of Dreamtime and the taste of roasted bogong
> moth.

Until the *Unnameable One* answers to all names,
called by quill whistle, hand-held drum,
dried gourd, springbok rattle,
and the low-pitched drone of the didgeridoo.

Lessons for a Young God

Goats

"The leopard shall lie down with the kid."
Isaiah 11: 6b

If we are to rest with leopards,
the child must give us claws,
or remove theirs —
give us speed,
or slow them down —
amend their taste for meat,
or ours for plants.

Lessons for a Young God

Song of Songs

*"I will get me to the mountains of myrrh,
and to the hill of frankincense." Song of Songs 4: 6*

"This is my beloved and this is my friend." Song of Songs 5:16

He is like an unbroke colt, long-legged and sleek,
who races full-tilt around the fields for no reason
but Spring, his hooves sending clods of sweet grass
skyward as he slows then spins near a filly whose
presence charges him with a curious new thirst.

It is time for him to go to the Mountains of Myrrh,
where lovers turn into gazelles grazing on lilies
and entire kingdoms float on the breeze—redolent
with warm cinnamon, saffron, and frankincense—
their undulating borders surveyed by birdsong.

There, all things are under the gaze of a woman,
beautiful and dark, who tends the vineyards high
on the Spice Hills. Refusing to sit behind lattice
waiting for suitors, she runs when she should walk,
turns her face to the sun unveiled, and chases foxes.

From her, he shall learn the language of desire inscribed
in a lush confusion of signs only the loins can decipher.
And when his lessons are done and he begins his work
to heal by touch, he shall feel her balm of words well up
in his hands: "This is my beloved and this is my friend."

Lessons for a Young God

The Heavens

"The heavens are telling the glory of God and the firmament proclaims his handiwork. Day to day pours forth speech and night to night declares knowledge." Psalm 19: 1-3

Alone in the night, the boy gathers our stars.
They have formed into a spiral galaxy
revolving slowly in his grass-lined basket.
Near the bottom, a pulsar chirps amid
the hum of interstellar background sound.

Light years condense to nanoseconds
as he plucks a black hole from our void and vault.
He holds it in his palm like a prized cat's eye marble
found in the dirt of a distant eon, then waves it
over the basket of stars. Their spectra quiver.
Fiery plumes illumine his face, and time blinks.

Come dawn, he releases them back to us,
one by one, like fireflies rising from a glass jar.
When his parents awaken, they find him asleep,
dreaming of firmaments beyond the scope of words.
While the dog star, happy to be set free,
trots amicably westward, catching a scent
on the morning air as if of Eden after the rain.

THE NATURE OF STONES

It was a great day to skip stones.
His personal best was one.

Cupped in a crucible of low hills, the lake
was molten copper flowing from the dawn sun,
but the water that lapped calmly at the boy's feet
was as cold as melted snow off Mt. Hermon.

He did not mind that his fingers were numb
as he searched for the perfect stone, flat and smooth
among the millions strewn on the beach,
weighing potential skippers in his palm,
envisioning each skimming above the lake,
walking three, four, five, six, seven steps,
to sink in triumph without any splash,
trailing into the depth bubbles of glee.

Finding one he thought would work, he tried
the sweeping side-arm throw that he had seen
the older boys use, instead of the bent-elbow,
over-the-shoulder toss of his yesterday's
younger self. The stone plunked, tossing up
a diadem of silvery droplets
reflecting the colors of lake and sky.
Unfazed, he tried again, with the same result.
So he sat down to think. Was it in the nature
of stones to skip? Did they sink for lack of skill?
Should he use a looser finger grip?
Should he flick his wrist before he let them go?

A gull landed beside the boy in hopes
that he had food to share, but when nothing
was offered, it flew off to catch a fish.
"If only I could change this stone into bread,"
the boy cried to the gull, "I would break off
a chunk to share with you." He closed his eyes
and imagined it turning warm and soft,
giving off the good smells of yeast and wheat,
but when he looked to see if it had changed,
all he saw was a pale gray stone,

striated with glimmering rose quartz,
as if the evenings and mornings of six days
had come to rest in the Sabbath of his hand,
and he saw that it was beautiful–and good.
"Catch yourself another fish," he murmured
to the gull hovering over the waters.
"I'd rather be changed into bread myself
than to change this stone into what it's not."
He watched the bird slowly circle around
and land nearby with a minnow in its beak.
"One day I'll change into a man, and that's enough.
I wouldn't mind if it were a man in whom
still lives a little skipping-stone boy,
who likes the grit of sand between his toes
and slips away from crowds whenever he can
to stand all alone on an empty beach.
Such fun we'd have, the man and me, and when
he's sad, I'd find him a stone and whisper
to him to let it fly, then watch it skip across the lake,
perhaps to land, at last, on the far shore."

He swept his arm out to the side and threw.
It skipped two times. "Did you see that?" He jumped
to his feet in elation, startling the gull
into flight. "Twice is one more than once!"
And he began to search for another stone
that held within itself the power
to skip three times, which was one more than twice.

PI

*"All who heard the boy were amazed at the
intelligence of his answers." Luke 2: 47*

The morning's lesson was on triangles.
Using various lengths of knotted string,
the carpenter methodically explained
the relationships between the three sides,
starting with equilateral triangles,
then progressing to isosceles.
But the boy, though outwardly attentive,
spent most of the time solving quadratic
equations in his head, while slowly tracing
recursive patterns in the dirt with his toes.

Half afraid of once again being asked
a question that he would not be able
to answer, or understand, the man paused
and wrapped the knotted string around his hand,
observing as he did so the wood curls
that nestled like little birds in the boy's
unruly, black hair. "What are you thinking
about?" he asked hesitantly, calling
to mind a prior lesson on circles
when the boy had wanted to know if it
were possible to trap the circumference
between the proliferating sides
of the inner and outer polygons,
and was there any end to the number
that uncoiled like a snake, its pattern
never repeating. To a carpenter,
a number was a tool, like a hammer
or saw, not a pre-existent object
waiting to be found between the wheel-spokes;
so he had asked the boy to explain it
to him as they sat beside each other
on the bench, the boy's legs swinging back and forth
like pendulums, his feet brushing the ground
on the downward arc, cutting parallel
lines in the sawdust that covered the floor.

This time, as he had before, he allowed
the boy to frame the question for himself,
neither pushing nor prodding, giving him
the opportunity to meander
through his inner universe of numbers,
undisturbed. "I cannot ask it unless
you look in, not out," the boy said at last.
"The real world makes it seem silly, as if
a camel were squeezed through a needle eye."
The boy waited until the man spread out
his hands in a father's sign of blessing.
"Imagine that I move towards you halfway.
I step again and again but each time
exactly half way, my stride shortening
from badger-length to mouse-length to ant-length,
always splitting the distance between us.
Would I ever reach you? Or consider
the string you hold. If it were made of air,
not linen, could I keep dividing it
in two? At the very end, would I
hold *forever* in my hands, or *nothing*?"

The man opened his eyes. For a long time,
he stared at the rough piece of string still wrapped
around his fingers as if it had been changed
into blue thread worthy of a prayer shawl.
"King Solomon, were he with us, would not
be wise enough to answer your questions.
Perhaps when you are older, you will be
able to answer them yourself." He patted
the boy on the knee. "Go outside and play
with your brothers. No more lessons today."
As the boy skipped out the door following
the sound of children's voices, a wood curl
floated off his hair and hovered like a
ruby-throated hummingbird borne aloft
by eddies of thought. Then it too was gone,
and in the calm that enveloped the man,

he laughed at the wondrous absurdity
of his attempts to teach the boy when all
he had to give were lengths of knotted string
and the chance to explore, unhindered
and alone, infinity's farthest edge.

THE TEACHER OF MADNESS AND MUSIC

*"He will be a man of sorrows and acquainted
with grief."* Isaiah 53: 3

Sunlight glinting off the lake lashed his eyes
as he peered toward the houses clustered on
the shore. Something was tormenting his inner
voices, as if sparks on the wind had kindled
fires on their tongues. A mob screamed at him
to hide among the tombs, but when he turned
that way, a gang, spitting obscenities,
brutally wrenched him backwards and sent him
careening down the hill toward the village.
Trying to mute the uproar in his skull,
he hurled handfuls of gravel into the air
in a furious assault on the sky,
all the time bellowing "Be gone, Be gone."
But the wind blew the words back in his face,
leaving only the smallest of voices
to thread through the gusts, and that one whispered *come*.

The village was deserted by the time
he reached the fishing nets hung out to dry.
Bread had been left to burn in the ovens,
and water gurgled slowly from the mouths
of discarded clay jars, spreading dark
rings on the earth. A broken cord dangled
from a fencepost, while the sound of frenzied
braying receded far down the beach.
The only person who remained behind
was a small boy sitting on a bench by
the open door of the carpenter shop,
humming softly to himself while trying
to carve a whistle out of a thin reed.

When the man saw him, his voices snarled,
unleashing a hornet's nest of curses
which swarmed toward the boy only to plummet
to the ground at his feet, wingless and cold.
Raging in dismay, the man flailed his arms
as his voices squabbled and hissed

"Why do you hurt us? Why do you hurt us?"
The words skittered over themselves like crabs
in a pail, ripping each other apart.

"I do not hurt you," the boy said simply,
without glancing up from his work. "Do you
know how to carve a flute? I'd like to carve
a flute, but when I tried before, the notes
didn't come out quite right. They sounded more
like the high-pitched squeals of newborn piglets."

"If it were not you, you would have fled like
all the others." The voices vibrated
like a carcass teeming with flies, then changed
pitch and sounded like slithering maggots,
the spitting of cobras, until the vowels
and consonants turned into a vast cloud
of stinging midges, that swirled over the street.

"How many people live inside your skull?"
the boy asked, while cutting a notch in the reed.
"A legion," they growled. "Our name is Legion."

"No it's not." The boy looked up and smiled
as if the man were trying to fool him.
"Everyone knows that your name is Samuel."

When the voices heard that name, the man's wounds
began to throb, and in desperation
he jumped wildly about, the broken
chain gouging into his leg, as they screeched
sarcastically at the boy, "If you are
the one to bring good tidings to Zion,
when will you bring good tidings to us?"

"Today I decided to make a whistle
instead, but listen." The boy blew into
the reed and a chirp came out no louder
than that produced by a baby sparrow.

"See?" Disconsolately, he cast it aside,
and bent down to pick up another reed
from a pile he had cut that morning,
and in so doing noticed the man's leg,
bleeding, inflamed and encrusted with sand.
"Does it hurt?" he asked, but he did not wait
for a reply. "Perhaps I cannot make
whistles and flutes very well, but I think
I can remove that chain. I'm not strong yet,
but it looks half-broken through already,
and besides, there is no one else around
to help. Wait while I get my father's tools."

And in that instant, the cacophony
in the man's mind was gone. He sat down
on the bench obediently, astonished
at the quiet procession of thoughts
coming one by one, then held very still
when the boy returned with hammer and chisel,
both looking gigantic in his small hands.

"How old were you when your voices moved in?"
the boy asked, while attempting to angle
the man's leg so that a link lay on the ground.

The man spoke slowly, pronouncing each word
as if he were freeing a cage of doves,
one bird at a time. "No older than you,
and like you, much loved, longing for the day
I could stand with the men to read Torah,
each word a refuge rising up from the scroll,
a refuge I was not allowed to reach."
The man began to cry, the tears cleaning
narrow paths across his cheeks to his beard.
"What sin did I commit before I knew
of sin? I must have done a thing depraved
to drain the All Merciful of mercy."

Sitting cross-legged on the ground, the boy
set aside the hammer and the chisel

to position the man's foot in his lap,
almost imperceptibly stroking it
as if calming a frightened animal.
"I am more cursed than Job who overlooked
the gift he still possessed — his mind, with which
he cried for reasons, though to me, Reason
alone would be consolation enough."

"I cannot heal you," the boy said, placing
the chisel against the link with great care.
"I think a day will come when I will know how."
He brought the hammer down and the link broke.
"Then I will drive them out and send you home.
Don't move yet," the boy stood up. "I'll be back."
And once again he disappeared inside,
returning with a bowl of water and cloth
with which he began to clean the raw flesh.

As he did so, the man picked up the reed
that the boy had left on the bench, uncut,
and ran his fingers along it slowly,
examining the pattern of its growth.
Suddenly panic contorted his face.
He jerked his leg away so forcefully
he sent the boy toppling backwards,
knocking the breath from his lungs.

Like nothing the boy had ever felt,
the weight of immense grief crushed his heart,
and he lay on his back too stunned to move,
looking up at the empty vault of heaven
where a sliver of moon floated in silence,
and beyond that—an eternity of stars.
"Your voices are returning, aren't they?"
he gasped, while trying to pull himself up.

"Yes." The man bent forward and in anguish
clenched his head in his hands, the sentences
coming fast this time. "They mutter and bite,
scratching and pounding on a locked door that

begins to splinter. But one thing before
they break out, and I can no longer speak
for myself." He thrust the reed at the boy.
"You asked if I knew how to make a flute.
There are notes inside this one, pure and clear.
I can hear them. Don't use your knife to carve
the outside. Use it to release the notes."
And he was gone, running up the street
as if demons were driving him with whips.

The boy watched him clamber up the hill
until he disappeared among the tombs.
Then he sat down and for a long time gazed
uncertainly into the reed, tipping
his head to the side and curling his toes
in the dust below the bench till wonder
dawned in his eyes. "I see the notes!" he cried,
and picking up his knife, he set to work.

IN AND OUT OF SEASON

"And he shall be like a tree
planted by rivers of water."
                        Psalms 1: 3

An old fig tree,
neither lovely nor large,
odd in only one way:
in and out of season
it bore just beyond
arm's reach
a few sweet fruit
for children who
dared to climb,
as if it flourished
in a warmer place,
by rivers of water
beneath a summer sun
that never dimmed.
Then one evening
it toppled to the earth
so softly no one heard it fall,
brought down by the weight
of a sparrow landing on its
topmost branch.

So the old man had stood
in the landscape
of the boy's everyday.
Now instead of shade,
there was a swath of sky
so startling in its vacancy
even the blue was gone,
leaving him no choice
but to take root himself,
in time to grant to all
who dared to climb,
in and out of season,
a few sweet fruit.

BY WATER AND BY SPIRIT

Before he sought the river's cool water
at the end of the afternoon to wash
away the sawdust that coated his arms
and hair like pollen, leaving his mallet
on an upturned manger in need of a leg,
and his adze resting on a half-formed yoke,
he had been whittling sheep so perfect
that when set down gently on the work bench,
they had begun to graze among the shavings;
and mosquitos that buzzed as he flicked them
loose from the pine with the point of his knife
to torment the rounded haunches of a bear
gnawing on fish bones no bigger than pins.
And when he had finished, he had taken
his own body in his hands, shaping himself
into an olive tree in early spring about to bloom,
which was what the dove had glimpsed
as it dropped down from the clouds,
seeking only a branch on which to rest.

THE HEALER

(Mark 5)

We need him in the E.R. now!
He's where?
The back ward again?
Those chronic care
patients can wait.
Drag him down here.
No excuses.
By God, if I had his gifts,
I'd know how to use them!
You heard about last week?
Rushing to the E.R.—
twelve-year-old girl,
car crash, hemorrhaging—
he stops to heal a woman
with fibroid tumors
who jostles him in the hall.
Just makes it here in time;
has us in a cold sweat.
The next day the girl's riding her bike
as if nothing had happened,
and he's skipped out again
to touch some old crazy
living under the bridge
with delirium tremens
and flash-backs of Da Nang.
And while he's gone,
that gang war erupts
and we're in a frenzy
of gunshot wounds.
If he'd been here,
no one would have died.
He has no sense of what's acute:
the loss of sight fifty years past
as crucial as today's cardiac arrest,
though the blind man long ago
became resigned to the dark.

If he'd only learn to let
well enough alone.
Go tell him it's urgent.
We need him in the E.R. now.

THE PHARISEES CONFRONT
JESUS IN THE COURT OF CAIAPHAS

We refuse a part
in your passion play.
Act all the roles yourself.
Be jeering bystander
and weeping friend.
Be centurion
and executed thief.
Use no nails,
no scourge.
Weave no
crown of thorns.
Hang in the sky
by force of will,
forsaken by God
who, like us,
declines to appear.
But first, think on this:
would you take the road
to the place of skulls
if you knew for sure
that the world will be
no better for your death?
Tomorrow—or eons,
Here—or in lands
beyond our maps,
clubs will crack
against bone,
and blood will trickle
from a child's ear
in your name, not ours.
Die, if you insist,
but do so without hope
of a third day.
Who can tell?
Love may echo
through the silence
of your last cry.

MESSAGE FOR JOSEPH OF ARIMATHEA

Already my eye sockets cup night.
Hurry, unfold your prayer shawl.
Smooth its tassels before the sun sinks.
Lay me aside in your tomb, without myrrh.

My body will await the shroud's embrace,
though what you find to wrap,
come dawn, will be a ripple of water
across the surface of a dry pool.

Go to your Sabbath rest.
Were there time enough
for you to embalm my heart
as if it belonged to a pharaoh,

your hands would touch nothing
behind my pried back ribs
but the warmth of grass
where a deer once curled.

The Hidden

Truly, You are a God who hides himself.
Isaiah 45:15

Rossler Attractor

Never reaching a steady state, the fractal is an example of deterministic chaos.

BABEL

"Let us build ourselves a city, with a tower
that reaches to the heavens, so that we may
make a name for ourselves and not be scattered
over the face of the whole earth." Genesis 11: 4

The demolition blast was so intense,
it blew away their common tongue.

Across the Plains of Shinar,
parts of speech shrapneled the ground.

Syntax rained down like gobs of tar.
Nouns whirled in vortices of brick dust.

Mute, the people stood owl-eyed
in a heavy ash-fall of vowels,

shielding themselves from verbs
that ricocheted through the hush,

while spores of language settled
on their hair–Algonquian, Basque,

Belorussian, Maori, Tamil, Aleut–
and sprouted into an unspoken longing

for empty homelands only distant offspring
would reach via land bridge or reed boat,

borne by a shock wave of syllables
and a hunger for a name older than words.

TRYING TO WRITE SAPPHICS IN ENGLISH

Classic verse forms scrape in a hard barbaric
voice that knows no other embedded rhythms
but its own short-long. Unforgiving bastard,
    all that I have now!

PREMATURE

Lord, while you and I walk
alone together
in this fragile dawn light
constricted by thick clouds,
let us talk of death,
father to father.

You are called Ancient of Days.
Fold to your heart my daughter
who is new of days.
When the clasp of tiny hands
loosens and love unlaces
from the strands of DNA,
gather her to yourself,
earth to earth,
heaven to heaven.

Quickly before time convulses,
teach me how to hear the sound
of skipping feet
when as yet they curl inward
too round to bear weight.
Teach me how to catch her laughter,
when the heart monitor no longer
traces a beeping line.

My God, I also am not ancient of days,
nor omnipotent, sometimes not even kind.
Give me the strength to incubate love
under these fierce lights
even when pain blooms.

RITE OF PASSAGE

We did not want to tell you we had no anchor out.
The line over the side was tied to a useless rock
that hung ten feet beneath the hull. Land was so far,
if land there was at all. There was no way to tell
if we drifted or stayed. The maps that we were left
seemed true at first but only led to different seas
with unnamed stars, while the compass was just a toy,
endlessly circumnavigating its own true north.
Now that you are old enough to understand,
we tell you sheepishly, embarrassed by our ruse,
but you would not have slept so sound through all those storms
had you realized we drifted without end. You thought
we stayed out here by choice. Now you know: we never knew
how to return, or if we wanted to.

DYSLEXIA

(for Marc)

November,
and the necromancer
dances
in your head,
changing b's
to d's
and six's
to nine's.
He sets
your hand
against
the tide
of left
to right
and hobbles
your feet
when you try
to run.

November,
and the necromancer
conjures snow.
While other
children skip,
you are
encrusted
with frost
and forced
to trudge.

November,
and the necromancer
conspires
with ice.

Though I
wrap my arms
around you,
I cannot
block
the cold.

AURORA BOREALIS

It started in third grade. Studying Eskimos,
we built igloos out of sugar cubes and set
them in a box covered with blue tissue.
Across the back we glued pieces of ribbon candy,
left over from Christmas, to be Aurora Borealis.
> The sound alone was wonder, more sung than spoken;
> evoking a goddess to a triune-bound class;
> commingling polar darkness and Mediterranean dawn.

Next came our Arctic phase. While cicadas
buzzed heat waves, we gnawed the leg bone
of our faithful husky, then lit our last match
at 80 degrees below, surrounded by the icy
reflections of undulating rainbows.
> Later, we imbibed facts: magnetospheric storms;
> Van Allen belts; solar winds streaming earthward,
> raining down electrons that collided into color.

But not until last night in this quiet April forest,
barren of leaves, had I ever seen it, glowing
like misplaced moonlight over a northern hill,
> only to mistake it for a spectral outrider of war.
> Shaking off the compression of trees, I climbed the rise,
> feeling exposed and uncouth, afraid my apprehension
> branded me an hysteric grinding her teeth on the hard
> consonants of Yucca Flats.

Suddenly the taut cloth of darkness ripped.
Light poured through each failed seam,
a luminous flood tide breaching the Milky Way.
> Feeling the release of a tenuous reprieve,
> I thought of the pipe cleaner Eskimo. Thirty years back
> in a blanched memory, he lifts a toothpick harpoon
> above a breathing hole, while unseen beneath the ice
> a killer whale rises.

A CHILD ASKS ABOUT DEATH
AND OTHER COMMON THINGS

(Written for an AIDS Healing Service)

One hundred years?
>   You too will be dead by then, my son,
>   and all that we have shared will be gone:
>   the way the light dapples the floor of your room,
>   the way I hum softly to myself as I work.
>   They will know other light and other rooms;
>   while we will be unfleshed figures in old stories.

What will be the same?
>   The expanse of sky, the bumblebee
>   buzzing against the window pane
>   and love climbing like a morning glory
>   round one generation to the next,
>   entwining each to each, higher, higher,
>   till the sun itself is bedizened with blue flowers.

What matters?
>   Did it wither in our hands or did we help it grow.
>   It makes no difference if they forget our names,
>   just as long as the love that took root a million years
>   before the first light fell on your face
>   sends out its tendrils for a million years
>   after the last light falls on mine.

THE CARTOGRAPHER OF DISASTER

"And he sent forth a raven and it went back and forth, to and fro, until the waters were dried up from off the earth." Genesis 8: 7

To traverse open water searching for signs of life,
a seabird is more suited than a land bird,
which needs the trustworthy stubble of wheat fields
and faithful hills that never drift to find its way.
But the raven, weak from long restraint, does its best,
trying to glide on stiff wings as the albatross
and seeking updrafts as the fish hawk.

First it scouts the contours of a submerged city
from which towers rise to the surface like waterlily stems
in a placid pond. Then it surveys a herd of ibex,
their recurved horns tangled in a mass of drifting reeds.
Expanding its search pattern, it marks the longitude
and latitude of a wine vat snagged on a pyramid's tip,
but nowhere does it see a single living thing.

Come nightfall, the raven, wing-weary and famished,
rests on the floating carcass of a bull elephant,
passing the time till dawn pecking topographic lines
into its bloated belly, pondering the great circle distance
of mud flats now turned into sea floor while grappling
with the problem of how to plot bearings as straight lines
that drowned mariners can follow to reach safe harbor.

When sunrise brings no hope of finding an olive branch,
the raven wonders what Noah will do with a damage tally
that includes a child's arm caught between fence posts.
Better to become a cartographer of disaster inking
a cartouche of ill omen than to return to the ark.
After all, what use are casualty figures to the dead
or promises of repair? Too late for them – rainbows.

EVEN THE BIRDS ARE BURNING
9/11

Too far away
to see
that wings were arms

feathers:

hair aflame,

what else could the child think
that clear September
morning
as she watched
incandescent
fledglings,
new to the wind,
plummet
down
gravity's airstream
past molten steel piers,
fissured glass

reflecting

blue?

"Even the birds are burning,"
she cried,
wondering
who would peck
the crusts of bread
she took to the park
each day
when there was nothing
in all the sky

but

sky.

Parched Wilderness

Remember him before the silver cord is severed,
or the golden bowl is broken; before the pitcher is
shattered at the spring or the wheel broken at the well,
and the dust returns to the ground it came from,
and the spirit returns to God who gave it.

Ecclesiastes 12: 6-7

Fractal Thorn

The Thorn patterns depend on whether, and at what speed, the
repeated functions escape to infinity.

ALTARPIECE FOR ALZHEIMERS

First Panel, Youth

Without leaving her side,
he has left her.
After fifty years of sleeping
beneath the same sunburst quilt,
he has re-crossed
the mountains of memory
      to his mother
      and the dark muck
      of Ohio bottom lands
      where asparagus pushes
      him out of bed each spring
      demanding to be cut
      in the yellow-pink
      of early dawn;
      to his brothers,
      evening dampness
      fuzzing their pomaded hair
      as they dare Prohibition
      in a Model T;
      to a Sabbath calm,
      his baritone throbbing
      what a friend
      he has in Jesus.

Dismayed, she watches his life
curl back on itself
and collapse inward,
sucking time with it,
until he is illumined
by an earlier light
in which she does not walk.

Second Panel, Adulthood

Shuffling round and round the house
in tattered slippers, he searches
for something, not knowing its shape
or size, only its lack. Driven
without any idea of where,
at least he has a lifetime
of practice in the knightly
art of the holy quest:
      over lunch break
      at the aircraft factory
      he treks into the tangled
      outback of faith,
      (a book on prophecy
      jostles with egg salad
      in his metal lunch pail);
      between singing hymns
      at the convalescent home
      and staking tomatoes
      in the sandy backyard,
      he seeks the divine
      via pamphlets he ordered
      from a TV evangelist,
      guaranteed and postage-paid,
      while the scoff of highballs
      and cold beer waits in the fridge.

For weeks now, he has been packing
for one last attempt; a single shoe,
his ukulele, a frayed wool hat,
a coat with a broken zipper
shoved in a worn-out suitcase.
When she is not looking, he slips away,
beyond reach by the time
she sets down her coffee cup.

Third Panel, The Inferno

In his cortex   one

more molecule   abrades

a seismic

jolt

the brain pan   cracks

memory shudders   tears loose

her face   disintegrates

the way back

collapses

cutting him off

even from him

self.

Fourth Panel, Purgatory

Repulsed by the emptiness
of the house now that he has
been sent away, she stands
on the front stoop sweeping up
pieces of a broken Christmas ball.
Curved golden shards snag
in the fringed doormat
along with strips of silver tinsel.
A cortege of dry leaves scratches
across the icy walk and snares
on the branches of the spruce,
which he always pruned
to a perfect conical shape

as if it were a pegboard toy.
She lights a cigarette,
shielding the match until
it burns down to her hands.

Fifth Panel, Death

She goes first.
From diagnosis to death —
three weeks;
doing crossword puzzles
to the last night,
at home, her voice
garbled by morphine.

Her daughter writes
the letters in the squares
using erasable ink,
vertical and horizontal
crossing into final
revelations.

Sixth Panel, Transfiguration

Shoveled into
his suit and tie
at the rest home,
he is told his Rose
has died and thinks
he has lost a flower.
Is told again, until
garden on garden
of roses vanish,
leaving behind
a petal trail across
the snow for him
to follow,
at last to find.

REST HOME GENESIS

Lord, on this day,
unnamed and unnumbered,
I feel you hovering
over my stagnant waters,
waiting to speak.

But how can you strike
star sparks
from the sodden
kindling of my heart?

How can you ignite
a sun from the rotting
wood of my soul?

For me, night leaches
into day, day seeps
into night, no separation
but shallow naps
in a straight-backed chair.

I grow old, old.
I have brought forth
according to my misbegotten kind
and they no longer care.
Love clots
on my lips like dried spit.
Darkness is on my face.

I fear that after endless
evenings, endless
mornings, your light
will break forth
on the void of cold,
closed eyes
and I shall not wake.

But if it must be so,
Oh, Lord, grant me simply this:
do not let me outlive

my longing for your word.
Then when my frayed
thread snaps,
I will know that it was
good.

CHAIN-LINK

Think of time before you knew the word for it,
when clock hands spun every which way, spewing
seconds like droplets from a sprinkler onto
your beribboned braids that streamed out behind you
as you skipped across the sun-flooded garden,
while on the surface of each second, light split
into a spectrum of possibilities
from unseen infrared to ultraviolet,
mottling the delft blue of the bindweed that
imperceptibly twined your ripening days
to a chain-link fence of Before and After,
until your years rattled in the wind like dried gourds.

COMING TO TERMS

He may never reach this mountaintop,
high above the ice-gouged valley, again.

Age is a heavy pack he cannot shed
and each day scours detail from his sight.

Dark trees blur into dark rock
and a crevasse blends into the shadow of a branch.

On a windy western ledge, he rests his knees,
which curtly remind him of a hundred other climbs.

Far below, a thin gold thread glints
through the dappled greens of spruce and oak,

while the White Mountains surround; to the east, the triple
peaks of Tripyramid beckon; to the north Mount Lincoln.

He wonders whether the thin gruel of memory will suffice
when the hunger for mountains begins to gnaw

and if he can summon the courage to unlace his boots
for the last time. Nearby at a precarious angle,

a glacial erratic sparkling with quartz leans
into the wind waiting for the return of the snows.

ELEGY FOR THE CATHEDRAL BUILDER

How dare you decamp with the work undone!

You, who carried the blueprints
unrolled in your chancelled brain,
have absconded with every rib,
vault, arch and flying buttress,

leaving me to hunker down—

an abandoned gargoyle with mortared feet,
her misshapen chin cupped
in little clawed fists,
who dreams of light

streaming through stained glass.

GRIEVING KNOWS NO DEARTH
IN ITS VERDANT SEASON

I will wait here next to the dried out stream bed.
I will rub chafed hands in the shade of boulders,
Holding cold hard words in my mouth, rough pebbles
     scratching my parched tongue.

     Grieving knows no dearth in its verdant season.

I am but a carapace filled with nothing.
Even love, which I was convinced I gave in
Priceless pure ore chunks, in this glaring noonlight
     proves to be fool's gold.

     Grieving knows no dearth in its verdant season.

Death has caused those near me to stutter harshly.
Vowels form clumps, consonants clink together;
Meaning, once so fluid, coagulates in
     pools in the voice box.

     Grieving knows no dearth in its verdant season.

Like a string cat's cradle, if–only thoughts loop
Back and forth: one web, then the second web and
Third till last meets first and becomes an endless
     snagging of taut threads.

     Grieving knows no dearth in its verdant season.

GAMING

On the day after Social Security checks
arrive in the mail, the casino is crowded
with elderly people, most of them at the slots,
whispering little prayers to the souls of Machines
for this once, *oh just this once*, a munificent
bleed of coins; while at the nearby museum,
children gaze at a diorama of an ice age hunt
in which Indians, with spears raised high, implore
the spirit of Caribou to give up its life,
to turn broadside; bones, joints and sinews rotating
into perfect alignment, the chance for one more chance.

GROCERIES

Some dreams are strong enough
to cross night's borders into day.
They tarnish the lettuce at the store,
darken the color of the ground meat,
and turn my shopping cart truculent.
Meathooked through my mind, they drain
me pale by the frozen foods.
And why are the peaches all bruised?
Were they damaged on the tree?
Or did a lackadaisical stock boy
drop them on the floor?
Either way, my dreams engorge their rot
with meaning past simple throw or fall.
I buy them with an empathy
not meant for fruit.

BLACK TEA

My black tea
      bought in Arizona
      brewed in New York
      by a family
      of Italian descent
      from leaves picked
      on Indian plantations
      by women workers
      whose wages have been cut
tastes of spring rain.

APOSTATE

My father's tent has collapsed.
The poles snapped in last night's storm.
The canvas flutters in shreds,
and the pegs, still tied to ropes,
lay wrenched from the earth.

Again the wind begins to rise.

Wordless, I wrap the torn cloth
around my shoulders,
and face the void of sky,
knowing that for sins of the spirit,
there is no redemption.

THE PURPLE LAMB

In a room of old women, the one in the first bed
cannot find amidst the rubble of her stroke-seized brain
any word but "home." Intoned, it sounds like "om,"
save for the phoneme "h" to which all meaning clings.
The patient in the second bed opens and closes her eyes
in rhythm with the soft drone, the motion of her lids
as slow as the tail flick of a tired fish swimming
in place within the murmur of a stream. Between them
a small boy swings his feet in the only visitor's chair,
holding a picture of a cotton-ball lamb with purple legs
tumbling off a cliff into the curve of a shepherd's staff
crayoned with a great sweep near the bottom edge.
Reluctant to give it to the one he loves but no longer knows,
he stares at the other woman's untouched lunch tray:
food cold, lid still on the coffee, utensils sealed in plastic,
an almond cookie in a fluted paper cup. Aware of his gaze,
she struggles to unfold her clenched right hand, thumb joint
creaking like a rusted hinge on a cathedral door,
until grasping the cookie, she lifts it by slow degree
as if offering up the host. Tipped towards him,
it trembles mid-air. He hands her the purple lamb in trade.

Void and Vault

And God said, "Let there be a firmament
in the midst of the waters, and let it divide
the waters from the waters.

Genesis 1: 6

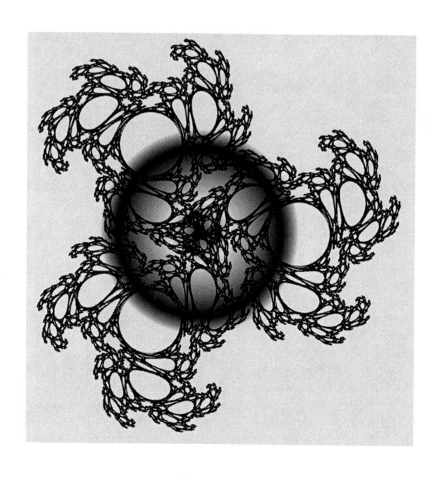

Twon Dragon

The Twon Dragon fractal evokes the Tai-chi symbol.

THE VOID AND VAULT OF HEAVEN

"I am not in a good place and I am no painter." Michelangelo

I. Adam

On the scaffold twenty meters up
tracing her head in the damp plaster,
Michelangelo knows it's going to take
more than a breath to make Adam drop
his can't-be-bothered pose, too bored
to stand even at God's charged arrival,
held aloft by a crew of hard-working cherubs
who struggle to maintain lift long enough
for contact to occur: a critical maneuver
of the right hand complicated by the added
weight of Eve on whom His left arm rests.
Paint freckles Michelangelo's face as he
wonders how many priests will take offense
but concludes that only skin to skin will do.
Without it, Adam's forever grounded.
God's touch is first. Hers is next.

The Void and Vault of Heaven

II. Body Parts

The trouble is the halo. He's never dissected one,
prying it open with a blade under cover of night
to determine its component parts: seeking with his
fingertips for the thin band of cartilage that holds
it erect, or the branched nerves channeling light
as coldly steady as foxfire on a rotting log.
The same goes for wings. Without evidence
from his cadavers, he dispenses with them,
painting angels as fit as young quarrymen
and pasta-loving cherubs to whom aerodynamic
principles will never apply. Even God looks
as if he climbs into bed each night stiff
from a hard day's work but not ready for sleep,
his brain crammed with thumb-nail sketches
of airy beings aglow with inexhaustible fuel
flying by faith in unborn Bernoulli's constant.

The Void and Vault of Heaven

III. Delphica

Ringed by water buckets and sacks of ash,
he yearns for the cool marble stacked in his shop
awaiting his touch to morph into warm flesh.
But the only way back is straight across
twelve thousand square feet of curved space,
troweled smooth one miserable day at a time.
Groaning as he prepares to traverse the section
allotted to Delphica, for whom he grinds pigments
(cinnabar, blue azurite, yellow ochre, burnt Sienna),
he envisions her as Apollo's girl, now widowed
and on her own, replacing riddles with straight talk,
who earned the right to look down on future popes
by foreseeing Christ in the vapors of the old gods.
He plans to imbue her with the strength to refill her
Parnassian spring, to see reflected thereon the face
of a man reaching up to paint her lips vermillion.

The Void and Vault of Heaven

IV. Self-Portrait

After four years, he has finally reached the end,
and now Jonah, whom he has reserved for last,
dangles his bare feet over the void, sharing
his precarious aerie with a dead fish, two cherubs,
and a vine, reclining on his arm and eying God
– a marvel of foreshortening – as if still arguing
petulantly that he is not the man to undertake
such a hare-brained job, lacking both talent
and inclination, his fingers pointing in opposite
directions, one to the threat of Nineveh and Rome,
the other to the safety of Tarshish and Florence,
regarding his own death as a small price to pay
to make a point. Yet as the fresco dries to stone,
he gazes beyond the gap between his intractable
pique and God's intractable grace, dumbfounded
at the resplendent vault arching above a city at peace.

STRANGE GRACE

Glacial ice fields sparkle
behind us.
In the spare serenity
of a level resting place,
we take off our gaunt packs
and stretch out our legs,
thigh muscles quivering
with the exertion of climbing
in thin air, untaught and without
rope.

Looking back, we see our tangled
footprints turn, stop, circle, and then
begin to lengthen,
as if sure,
before halting abruptly
on the edge of a chasm
we never saw, nor sensed,
changing direction
and stumbling across a snow bridge
so fragile it collapses
under the weight
of a sunbeam as we watch,
all hidden in the long darkness
through which we had no choice
but to move,
desperately praying our way,
each word ice-axed into the side
of God.
Squinting into the fierce glare,
we locate our small snow-covered cairns,
built of rock and chunks of hacked out frost,
marking where others mis-stepped
and fell.
We who have made it across are a smaller crew,
and more lean,
knowing it was not skill, or luck,
that brought us here,
but some kind of strange
grace.

We remove the crampons,
hoping we have no more need,
but knowing there is no sure footing,
nor ever has been,
the way forward as dangerous
as the way back,
but in this moment of clear, high light,
as we study where we have been,
we are awed at the other tracing in the snow,
near to our steps, as if of
wings.

IN THE BEGINNING OF THE BEGINNING

In the 10th century,
a Persian astronomer
named *The Mystic*
looked beyond the Milky Way
into deep space
where he observed
a "nebulous star"
north of Delta Velorum,
a discovery that had to be taken on faith
until the 17th century
when a German astronomer
glimpsed through his telescope
the Andromeda Galaxy
glowing like the "light of a candle
seen through a horn."

So also a Hebrew poet,
who saw the unseen
in the dark vault of the cosmos,
coiled into language
an intimation of relativity
long before e's, m's, c's and superscript 2's
permutated to theory in
Einstein's head.

How else to explain
the creation of *light* prior to any source,
space unbounded by mass,
time without a way to mark its passage?

How else to explain
velocity wavering over the deep
until it congealed into the first particle of sand
on the first beach?

How else to explain
that before teeth fissioned the apple
and loosed devastation from its core,
God looked out and saw
Good,
unsplintered and sweet,
in the beginning of the
Beginning?

AN ASTRONOMER'S PRAYER

"What are humans that you are mindful of them?"
               Psalm 8: 4

My Cosmological Constant,
some say:
>   I am nothing
>   but a virtual particle
>   with a mass so light
>   and a time so short
>   I am gone before I am;
>   and you are nothing
>   but the alpha and omega
>   of natural law;
>   and I am nothing
>   but an infinite bubble
>   snagged on a finite nail;
>   and you are nothing
>   but a refracted thought.
Yet no one can say:
>   on what scale I should weigh
>   the dark matter of my life;
>   which geometry best explains
>   the dimensions of my heart;
>   and why when your love flared
>   like a supernova across time,
>   unbent and unbending, it rode
>   by choice Earth's gravitational
>   current to here, to now, to me.

BIG WORD/SMALL WORD

My childhood was tinctured by the big word
    predestination,
which my Sunday school teacher struggled hard
to explain against the roar of the boilers in the
overheated basement of the Presbyterian church.
Under the caged lights and ragged basketball nets,
she managed to impress on me that I already
had a first-class train ticket to heaven in my pocket
(along with gum, a lace hanky and a cat's-eye marble).
At ease with my election, which I vaguely connected
with voting for President Eisenhower, I ducked
spit balls tossed across the round wooden table
into which initials, some in heart-framed pairs,
were carved so deeply that when I tried to color
a picture of Jesus, my crayon jolted outside the lines.

My neighbor's childhood was tinctured by the big word
    transubstantiation,
that, according to her, was a kind of okay cannibalism
taught by strange birds in black robes and winged hats
who roosted in something called a parochial school.
·These dark creatures also told her I was going straight
to Hell, which was alright with me because I was sure
that she was going there too, since she had no ticket
in her pocket, and we'd have each other to play with.
But she said Hell was terrible, and anyhow, she *did so*
have a ticket stamped by some old man named Pope,
who my mother explained was Italian, signifying to me
meat balls, pizza, and foreign babies with pierced ears.
An uneasiness settled on us. We found new playmates.

Not until we were teenagers did we learn the word
    ecumenism,
and for the first time she came to sock hops in the church
basement, doing the stroll over the center court line,
and I began to wave hello to the nuns who waved back.
I crumpled up that predestination ticket and threw it away.

And when a few years later the Civil Rights movement
swept over us both, we linked our arms together and sang
"We Shall Overcome," transubstantiating into it the small word
friend.

WRESTLING WITH AN ANGEL

So Jacob was left alone, and a man wrestled with him
till daybreak. When the man saw that he could not
overpower him, he touched the socket of Jacob's hip
so that his hip was wrenched...But Jacob said
"I will not let you go unless you bless me."

Genesis 32: 24-25

Tell me quickly: beyond
which turn in the road
is the view back all regret?
Is it soon? Are there signs?
Will I reach it unawares,
too late to turn around,
or shout a warning
to those who come behind?

I will not let you go
until you speak.
Will I walk this road
dragging a sack
of wasted gifts,
not lifting my head
for fear of learning
I shuffle in place?

Or worse, will I strew
my discontents across
the way like tacks,
forcing sons to veer,
daughters to plod, or stop?

If that is what will be,
then while it is yet dark,
this is the blessing I demand:

> Do not just touch my hip.
> Shatter me!
> Leave not one bone dangling
> from its socket,
> not a single curving rib.

Leave nothing at all
but the absolution of dust
kicked up by a child
skipping on a daybreak road
that never felt my step,
while overhead a finch
warbles matins. Oh angel,
bless this usurper of blessings:
Shatter me now.

MISERERE

Lord, ream out my ears so I cannot help but hear
your razored voice slicing across the thin edge of silence.

Against my will, wrench me from lukewarm Laodicea
where I lounge in the ease of my faith. Blister my soul

      with the searing winds of evening news hot spots,
      or else I will be like them who refused to inhale
      the smell of the ovens in which Jews burned.

You, whose love is not tame, let me feel the crack
of your shepherd's staff across my head.

For my pain, let there be no salve but you.
For my shelter, let there be only the shadow of your wing.

      For my food, let me come to the table you prepared
      in the presence of my enemies and find nothing to eat
      until I realize that it is they who must be fed.

Then when you have gouged from me the carefully wrought
deception of my worth, thrust in its place the live coal
with which you singed Isaiah's lips, until my words glow
with an incandescence no still waters can quench.

PRODIGAL

How many times,
in those years I called you Father,
did I still with my fist
the flutter of your Spirit's wing,
pommel your gentle voice
silent,
and spit out the wick you kept
burning in the night
in case I should wake
frightened?

Having blindfolded
and gagged my captious soul,
so it could only mew sightless,
how was I to know
you waited by the road,
years and years,
longing for my return?

I stand before you now,
shoeless in the dust,
reeking of pigs,
to ask no epiphany,
no cataclysm of mercy.
Do not lift from me the agony of truth:
Father,
I have not loved you enough—
and never will.

TENTH MUSE

The sap in me dried up as in summer drought
Psalm 32: 4

This morning—
when self is thick
with discouragement
and ready to abandon
poetry—
Sappho suddenly appears.

With saffron hair
garlanded with violets,
she steps across a Pacific of time
as if it were nothing but a small freshet
created by the softest of spring
rain.

In mime,
I offer her tea
but she insists instead
on sipping the golden sunlight
that spills across
my hands and arms.

In the blue flames
beneath my teapot,
I see her poems catch fire
as jubilant priests in hair shirts
hitch up their robes to dance
glorias.

A singed scrap flutters upwards
in the heat waves
and settles beside my cup:
    "it is not right for grieving
to abide in the dwelling place of
poetry."

Knowing that the tiny inner pool
where poems spawn
is drying up,
she hands me a small green flute
from which words fall
like raindrops.

POETRY'S IMPERATIVE

As someone who is freezing to death
breathes on sparks set to tinder in cupped hands,
you breathe across your words;
too strong a breath, or too soft, and nothing ignites,
dead galaxies in a dead universe.

Around you shiver the words of poets
with unpronounceable names,
in untranslatable dialects
printed in phantom inks on acid-based paper,
decaying even as you compose.

While insistent of sound, in your ear
a Tatar reed whistle plays as Ts'ai Yen sings
of banishment to China's northern wastes,
waving a willow leaf over her head
as her sons dim to sparks in her iced eyes.

Toward the end of the Second century C.E., Ts'ai Yen, an important Chinese poet, was captured by the Tatars and taken north. There she bore two sons to a Tatar leader before being ransomed back to China, leaving her sons behind. In "Eighteen Verses Sung to a Tatar Reed Whistle," she wrote that as her sons vanished into the distance, her soul was overwhelmed by the separation. All she had left was her poetry.

EMAIL FROM ORACLE BONE TO ARTIFICIAL INTELLIGENCE

From/To/Attach/Subject

I begin with *From*
before the first backslash,
meaning origin or source,
an appropriate word,
for I am an oracle bone,
a scapula really, all
that remains of an ox,
a plow-pulling placidity
that, massively unfleshed,
is useful for divination,
having reached maturity
without the distracting
essentials of desire.

To questions entered
with the point of a blade
during the Shang dynasty,
I gave yes-no answers
translated by monks
who read the binary code
of my heat-fissured cracks.

But just as sentience,
the *Subject* of this email,
can be defined as the power
to be contrary, the same
is true for an oracle bone
cogitating on a cold hearth
in Boolean mindfulness

divining you, the *To*,
an artificial intelligence
so distant and all-becoming.

And what was my answer
to King Wu Ding who asked
three thousand years ago,
"In ten days no disaster?"
I replied, "No," then *Attached*
"But perhaps alarming news."

One of the earliest forms of writing is found on oracle bones, which were either tortoise shells or scapulas used for divination. The question and answer in the last stanza are incised in the oracle bone Ching-hua 2.

BIRD DANCER

When I was small,
I dreamed of dancing,
swirling so perfectly through the air
gravity couldn't bear
to pull me
down.
Every muscle hummed.
Every cell kept time.
I was a swallow-child playing on the
wind.

Even now I strain
over these words
like a dancer chained
to the bar,
yearning to leap
free.

Above my head
ideas twitter,
kept aloft
by gleeful syllables.
They catch a thermal and rise.
Look, the sun glints through their
wings.

Consider Thy Heavens

*When I consider thy heavens, the work of thy fingers,
the moon and the stars, which thou hast ordained,
what is man that thou art mindful of him?*   *Psalm 8: 3*

Inside-Out Dragon

The fractal is calculated according to how quickly it moves beyond
perception.

THE SPEED OF LIGHT

If I were to tell you
that light can be slowed
from 186,000 miles per second
to 38 miles per hour
by firing lasers at a condensate of sodium atoms
chilled to 50 one-billionths of a degree
above absolute
zero,

which is the truth,

I would also tell you
of a winter's night,
and a white horse
galloping
along a snow-covered ridge,
mane and tail
streaming out against the sky
like Chinese brush strokes
across black
silk,

and as it runs,
it scatters ice crystals
that glint like fiery suns,
while the moonlight cascades
into its hoof prints
and freezes into sapphire
pools,

which is the truth,

then I would leave it to you
to ride
the particle of the first
on the wave of the second
into a landscape
where truth
is light in all its forms
at once,

including the glimmer
in memory's condensate
of a luminous
horse
slowing near the crest
to whinny at the
stars.

THE FOOL JOTS DOWN A BEDTIME PRAYER

Lord, you know my mind
and all its convolutions;
how all things are lost,
and nothing;
every forgotten moment
of the hand, the eye,
incorporated
into the way I
comb my hair, the slant
of these words across the page.

If you dredged the bottom
of my brain, what ancient things
would be unearthed?
Crayon marks in primary colors
scribbled by a two-year-old
on the inside of my cranium?
Deeper and older,
drawings of extinct bison
on dark artery walls?
Veins clogged with primordial ooze?

Since I do not know
the composition of my mind,
just how am I supposed to pray?
The language spoken by saints
is to me an unknown tongue,
as foreign as the glottal click
of Folopa hunters in the
rain forests of New Guinea,
as lost as Ugaritic etched into
shattered stone stellea.

All my meanings tangle
as rhizomes in sod
beneath the rustle of prairie grass.
If only one word,
like a blade of little blue stem,
could break through,
one pure word pulling
clods of metaphor into your sight,
I think I could lay-me-down-to-sleep then,
and leave it to you to whistle up the morning.

STAR FALL

I believed what I was taught about the stars,
how they were suns light years away from earth,
not lamps affixed to creaky astral orbs,
or bears, plows, scales, and gleaming pearls.

I knew them by their vestigial names.
White dwarf: a little malformed man
grinding bones in a dark medieval wood.
Red giant: a swollen cyclops going
blind in his bloodshot eye.

> But then it
> fell
> on my lawn,
> a pure
> white thing
> with icy
> points.

I picked it up, my fingers incandescent
as if the glow were kindled in my bone.
Foreseeing the rubble of our cosmology,
pre-formed questions tangled in my brain.
Was it alive? Did it have a weapons use?
And what would happen if fed to mice?

Should it be splintered among a thousand labs
until only a sparkle was left upon my hand?
What would become of those refusing to recant
their belief in pulsars, quasars, novas?

Would they crawl inside their telescopes to die?
All the answers I could construct were flawed.
So after one last look, I threw it back.

It rose unmindful
of parabolic curves
and gravity's pull
until piercing
the black vault,
it twinkled.
Around it I watched
the Pleiades dance.

FOLK WISDOM

When satellite data on cloud cover and water vapor
revealed that perturbations in ocean temperatures
can cause high cirrus clouds to dim constellations
in the Southern Hemisphere, it proved what Andean
farmers have known since Inca time: the day to plant
potatoes is foretold in the sky far ahead of spring.
Bundled against the winter cold, they gather deep
in the night each June to study a cluster of seven stars
dangling low over the outline of the darkened Earth.
When smudged as if by smoke or mist, it warns of drought
and cautions delay. They call the coming year El Niño
after the Spaniards' child-god, born in a faraway land
in need of rain. Survival is the only proof required.

A SINGULARITY

And the power
that was always
everywhere
yearned
to think
one thought
at a time;
to taste
a kumquat
instead of
a cornucopia
of fruit;
to stroke
the nap of
ultraviolet
swaddling
the spectrum's
edge;
to watch
a wave of light
pool on
a particle of leaf.
So it dreamed
an evening
and a morning,
imagined
the number
one,
and became.

MEMO FROM THE METAPHOR EXCHANGE

And on the first day of the first month,
you shall trade in theological metaphors
(worn-out knees and baggy about the hips)
for their recycled opposites, pre-shrunk:
e.g., you who picture faith as a serene journey
shall be jolted by revelation;
you who perceive of heaven as a twilight garden
shall be pitched into the glare
of the Holy City's thronged streets.

Drawing you into unfamiliar sacred space,
these imperfect figures of speech shall tink
new riffs on the consonants of the silent
Name, each note a tiny seed taking root
in your churned up earth to sprout epiphanies
of blueprints for ruined cities rebuilt
where justice shall bloom like alabaster
on the banks of a torrent of light
in which metaphors, like patched jeans, come clean.

THE FOOL THINKS ABOUT LOVE

Go ahead, compare it
to a splendid bird,
or say it is a pure note you heard
drifting
with the snowflakes
on a winter's night.

I will compare love
to the lowly worm,
resurrection's workman,
who can transform dead flesh
into topsoil sprouting life,
who inherits
the tired earth and all
its rotting things
and makes them one.

Nature's slimy alchemist
whose gold is loam
is more like it:
for though love cannot create,
the heart's soil
it can rejuvenate.

THE FOOL CHATS WITH DARWIN

I beg to differ, Charles:

the human evolutionary line did not begin with apes
but with a pair of naked vegetarian gardeners who chose
to become carnivores after deducing that apple trees
required too much knowledge to grow, reverting
to sour little things, *Malus malus*, if not grafted.
It required a botany degree just to recognize the types:
Granny Smith, Winesap, Rome Beauty, Northern Spy;
which were good for pies and which for nothing but vinegar.
Now if they'd planted zucchini, a most redundant vegetable,
I think they'd be in Paradise still, naturally unselected,
and you would not have sailed to the Galápagos on the Beagle.

As to your ideas about gradual change—wrong again,
though who am I to say? And yet I am inclined to think
it didn't take them long to learn that hunting was hard.
They must have chipped a heap of flint before achieving
their first Clovis point. I can imagine them, furred and smooth,
with a variety of cranial shapes, trying to decide how heavy
the spear shaft must be to pierce a wooly mammoth's hide,
while telling their hungry offspring about a beautiful garden
and the god who walked there in the cool of the evening.
Evolution being what it is, even the god may have changed:
arms and legs becoming prehensile like those of the whale.

Take it from whence it comes, Charles.

BEATITUDE

so blessed am i

my soul does cartwheels

spilling love

like pink blue and green

jellybeans

from my patched pockets

heels up

head down

head up

heels down

until giddy and giggling

i sprawl

in the deep grass

of God's grace,

knocking the crescent moon

askew.

SOUL SEARCH

At what kink in the double helix does sentience occur?
In a photon-flash of Heisenberg uncertainty,
do amino acids ask existential questions?
Do stem cells dream?

Steeped in evolution, "red of tooth and claw," I seek
a gap, no wider than the edge of Occam's razor,
amid my competitive genes where transcendence
can spiral into immanence, like a tired fox

curling its tail around itself within the hollow
trunk of a chestnut oak as the evening stars appear,
while the bewildered howls of the hunting hounds
diminish down the valley and over the far hill.

ADAM DREAMS OF DARWIN'S FINCH

It descends in a cascade of feathers,
brushing his cheek with its wing tip,
one more bird of the air seeking a name.
He has identified so many varieties already,
he suspects they keep getting back in line,
each time slightly changed: beaks enlarged
to crack thistle seeds, talons curved
to clutch fish. Even in his sleep they come,
one by one, and always he feels a tiny flutter
in his throat, followed by a surge of syllables
lifting off his tongue, like a flock of geese
startled from the surface of a dark lake.
Yesterday it had been the arctic tern,
dropping out of the sky like a snow squall,
and before he sensed the tickle of words,
his eyes flooded with glacial melt water
and he felt on his palm the indentation
of a reindeer hoof under the pale light
of the polar sun. The day before, a pair
of rose-breasted grosbeaks had settled
on his shoulders, whistling of orchards
and sweet, bruised windfall a hum with bees.
The female, at first mistaken for a finch,
whirled in him such a flurry of longing
that he ran his thumb down its speckled
side while its name formed in his mouth.

Weary of learning the language of wing beats,
the rising inflection of the curlew's lonely cry,
the great horned owl's night-draped hoots,
Adam turns on his side and winces in pain.
In his dream, his arms wrap around skin soft
as eider down, of the kingdom Animalia, class
Vertebrata, of the order Primates, genus Homo,
species *sapiens* meaning wise, meaning woman,
as the finch pecks loose the jesses on his wrists,
and he flies.

KADDISH FOR LEVIATHAN

Of God's daily schedule,
unbroken throughout time,
the Rav wrote in the Talmud
that when His work is done,
He plays with Leviathan.

Is it a Narwhal playing
ring toss with its spiral tusk
under the wavering spectra
of the Northern Lights?
Or perhaps a Great Blue
that appears late each day,
when the ocean is languid
under slanted sunbeams.
Maybe it extends a fluke
for God to grasp and together
they sound into the abyss,
trailing silvery bubbles
as oxygen is compressed
in blood-warmed lungs,
till deep in the cold domain
of the giant squid
and coelacanth,
they turn and surge up,
shattering the eye of heaven.
Or is it a little Beluga
that fetches a stick thrown
in a high spinning arc
from the edge of the pack ice?

But it is also written that
there is only one Leviathan,
God having killed its mate
on realizing their offspring
would overwhelm the seas.

And so as dusk broods
over the waters,
they stop their play
while around them names
of extinct creatures float
like clouds of plankton:
great auk, saber tooth,
Neandertal, Homo sapien,
till with a shudder of fin,
Leviathan sinks into the sea
as God recites
the mourner's Kaddish,
plangent as whale song,
faraway and lone.

DARK ENERGY

"Behold, I create new heavens and a new earth." Isaiah 65: 17

A universe of sand and one river, its source obscured in mist,
should have sufficed as a royal domain were it not for rumors
that the land was ringed by water, enticing the pharaoh to hire
Phoenicians, with their uncanny sense of coastlines, currents,
riptides and winds, to circumnavigate Africa in their keeled boats,
starting from the Red Sea and returning via the Pillars of Hercules,
about which Herodotus wrote with disbelief due to a wild claim
made on their return that the sun was "on their right hand,"
meaning it traversed the northern sky, proof in retrospect
that they had crossed the Equator, for which their cosmology
could not account—an amazement now shared by astronomers
who, on studying the spectra of exploding stars, were stunned
to discover galaxies are flying apart at an accelerating rate,
as if, during a change in the night-watch, the ordered heavens
had morphed into a wastrel sky strewn willy-nilly with hidden
dimensions and disconcerting densities, leaving them no choice
but to seek the existence of what can't exist: dark energy,
repulsive gravity, massless neutrinos oscillating into mass;
much as the Phoenicians, unnerved more by the disappearance
of the Pole Star than the errant course of the sun, wondered
with dismay if they had outsailed the realm of their old gods
as they anchored each night under a sky gone utterly strange.

RIVERBED

I am a riverbed.
Nothing in myself:
a barren swath of gravel,
sand and stone;
a parched gully.
I offer no shelter
from the sun's heat.
I hold no fish
for the scavenging bear.
I am a riverbed,
hard, dry and still.

But give me some water
and I make it jump.
Flecked with mica,
my stones scatter light.
Here otters somersault;
there waterbugs dart.
My current strokes
a salmon's back.
I overflow my banks.

Lord, I am a riverbed.

Now bring on the rain.

Author

Kathleen L. Housley's poetry has appeared in *The Christian Century*, *Image: A Journal of Art, Faith, Mystery*, *Terra Nova* (MIT Press), and *Nimble Spirit* (online). She is the author of three acclaimed biographies: *The Letter Kills But the Spirit Gives Life: The Smiths* (Historical Society of Glastonbury); *Emily Hall Tremaine, Collector on the Cusp* (University Press of New England); and *Tranquil Power: The Art and Life of Perle Fine* (Midmarch Arts Press), chosen by *Choice Magazine* as one of the best academic books of 2005. She lives in Glastonbury, Connecticut.